Odd Topics
A Biblical Handbook For Weird Questions

D1526957

Written by Laura Danley

Illustrated by Mary Lou Cowden

Beloved, do not believe every spirit, but test the spirits to see whether they are from God, for many false prophets have gone out into the world.

1 John 4:1

Contents

First, the Gospel...

The Gospel is solid, unchanging, and unwavering. The truth is, we are sinners in desperate need of a Savior. Jesus is that Savior. He is the "Word" we read of in John 1:1 where it says, "In the beginning was the Word, and the Word was with God, and the Word was God." (John 1:1, NKJV) He was immaculately conceived, born of a virgin, and lived a sinless life despite being tempted as we are. Still, he willingly paid the price for all of our sins on a cross where He allowed himself to be crucified: "...being found in human form, he humbled himself by becoming obedient to the point of death, even death on a cross." (Philippians 2:8, ESV) Then, just as we celebrate every Easter - between the jelly beans, the Easter Bunny, and a Sunday service - Jesus left the tomb, alive. He rose from the grave and conquered death. If you are reading this book, you've probably heard all this before. I hope you believe it. If not, know that "...there is salvation in no one else, for there is no other name under heaven given among men by which we must be saved." (Acts 4:12) Therefore, this book begins from this premise - knowing that any truth, any hope, stems from a relationship with Jesus   Christ.

A Little Background:

An Encounter With a Coffee Mug

In 1999, I was nineteen and a staunch atheist. My faith hung on hard science; but like many teenagers, my quest for truth occasionally led me to crack open doors to the esoteric and peek outside the norm. Still, I was not expecting (nor was I prepared for) the following experience.

My friend and I were sitting at a booth in a local diner, as we had often done since high school. A group of young adults, similar in age, had taken the booth across from us. Nothing, it seemed, was out of the ordinary. Suddenly, as I was glancing in the other booth's direction, I saw a coffee mug slide across their table.

My glance became a stare. Each member at the table had their arms crossed. How, I wondered, did that happen? I decided that I had misinterpreted some visual cue, and went about conversing at my own booth. The coffee mug, however, continued to slide back and forth. The people seated at the table seemed unimpressed, as if they were watching this mug pinball around because they had nothing better to do.

I told my friend that I couldn't sit by and watch anymore. I crossed the aisle and asked them, "How are you doing that?" They let me look under their table and scrutinize their booth as the coffee mug skated from one direction to the next. I couldn't figure it out. I was dumbfounded.

At last, a young blonde man asked me, "Do you want to try?" I don't quite recall what I was thinking at that moment, other than knowing that I was overwhelmed with curiosity. They sat me down and taught me how to move the coffee mug with my "energy." Or at least, that's what they said it was. (I am now convinced it was demonic activity.)

My friend watched on, with hardly a care. The waiter walked over and briefly commented on the normalcy of the moment, too. It was as if the whole world knew about "magic" but me!

The foundation of everything I thought I knew was shaken that day. Without missing a beat, the young man that "taught me" to use "magic," took a vested interest in me - but he was very secretive. I know little about him today. I knew little about him then. I remember him discussing a local coven, but I don't remember his name or much else about the event.

Over the next several days, strange things began to happen. I had a low-budget apartment by the university, where I lived alone. However, I started to sense that someone was in the apartment with me. I'd never felt this way in my apartment before the coffee mug incident.

One night, as I sat in my room crying over who-knows-what, my phone rang. When I answered, the young man from the diner immediately said, "What's wrong?" No "Hello." No, "Hi, it's me." Just an immediate inquiry into why I was crying.

About this time, it became clear to me that he had been watching me, somehow. My boyfriend, at the time, told me I needed to get away from this group of people. Even he, an atheist himself, knew something wasn't right. I don't remember how I asked, but I asked the young man to stay away. Just like that, the feeling of an extra occupant in my apartment disappeared. Shortly afterward, I joined the military in an attempt to get my life on track; and when they asked me what religion I wanted to put on my dog tags I answered, "No Religion."

If you're already convinced that I'm mad, I don't blame you. However, if you've experienced some strange or even terrifying/uncomfortable things after being exposed to the occult, hear me when I say that you are not the only one that has experienced these things. The Bible tells us, "Your adversary the devil prowls around like a roaring lion, seeking someone to devour" (1 Peter 5:8). I didn't understand, then; but I see it now. I was being "devoured."

Over time, I began to experiment with other things, like spirit boards and tarot cards. Eventually, I could no longer refer to myself as an atheist. I knew there had to be something else going on, behind that which we see, and I wanted to know more. I wanted the truth, but I also wanted to be in charge.

So, I read every book about witchcraft that I could get my hands on, and I believed everything they told me. "Naive" doesn't begin to describe my behavior. I was a prodigal child and a fool. Perhaps that's why I was invited to a high priestess' house. I don't remember what the event was, but there were lots of people. I met local witches, and I thought I was finally connecting with like-minded people in the community. The high priestess told us about a "Wicca 101" class that she would be hosting. Like any decent overachiever, it was hard to get me to go away, and I pleaded to join the class. For some reason, though, they never let me. So, I continued as a solitary witch. Despite being allowed to attend esbats, I longed for companionship; and as my stack of books grew, so did my level of confusion.

In the summer of 2005, I realized that I would believe just about anything my books about Wicca told me. It was an eye opening moment, when I realized what a simpleton I had been. Everytime I had been exposed to a coven, I felt special - like there was something powerful about me, and it was addictive. It fed the ego, and gave me the illusion that I had some sort of power in my life, but as I turned away from the occult, I learned that I wasn't special. I was gullible, befouled, and stained.

That summer, some local Christians helped me get rid of every book about witchcraft and occult-oriented trinket in my house. From what I'm told, they had a big bonfire and burned all of it. While that was taking place, I got saved in a parking lot outside a local church. I realized that I was terribly lost in my sin and rebellion against God, that I needed a Savior, and that Jesus thought I was worth dying for - that He'd been watching out for me all along, even at my worst. All those spiritual doorways I threw open haphazardly were suddenly and solidly shut tight. I was sealed by His Holy Spirit, and all the otherworldly psychical torture stopped.

Thoughts on Heaven and the Spiritual Realm

According to *Strong's Concordance*, the ancient Hebrew word for heaven in Genesis 1:8 is *shâmeh*. It refers to the visible sky where air, clouds and even celestial bodies move. We are told "And God said, "Let there be an expanse in the midst of the waters, and let it separate the waters from the waters." And God made the expanse and separated the waters that were under the expanse from the waters that were above the expanse. And it was so. And God called the expanse Heaven. And there was evening and there was morning, the second day." (Genesis 1:6-8 ESV)

It could be argued that the waters above the expanse encompass the universe, and the waters below the expanse involve the earth we walk on; but, what if the sky is all part of the heavens labeled in the *expanse* and there is something beyond the familiar heavens? What if the universe, as we know it, is a part of the boundary that separates us from eternity? Afterall, how can the second law of thermodynamics -- how can entropy -- death, decay, decline -- possibly affect eternity? Eternity must be beyond the *expanse*, or somehow separate from our material realm -- but you already know that.

Imagine, if you haven't already, an omnipresent, omniscient, omnipotent Creator living outside our closed system (a.k.a, the universe). He's so powerful, and so different from anything we know that it's possible to believe that He *created* physics. He created time and space, matter and all that entails - but He is not susceptible to the laws of physics. We are, because we are His creation.

In other words, as we consider the odd topics in this book, remember not to put God in a box. He created the box, and we are in it. He is not. I'm not privy to all the facts about eternity. In fact, we have all been given the same resources in the Bible and the Holy Spirit. I don't have any special knowledge. So, let's look at what the Bible says about this *other place.*

In John, chapter 8, Jesus says in verse 23, "You are from below; I am from above. You are of this world; I am not of this world." In the Old Testament, at the Tower of Babel, Genesis 11:7

reads, "Come, let us go down and there confuse their language, so that they may not understand one another's speech." Psalm 103:11 says, "For as high as the heavens are above the earth, / so great is his steadfast love toward those who fear him..." In the story of the resurrection, we are told, "And behold, there was a great earthquake, for an angel of the Lord descended from heaven and came and rolled back the stone and sat on it." (Matthew 28:2) In Revelation 4:1 and 2, John writes: 'After this I looked, and behold, a door standing open in heaven! And the first voice, which I had heard speaking to me like a trumpet, said, "Come up here, and I will show you what must take place after this." At once I was in the Spirit, and behold, a throne stood in heaven, with one seated on the throne.'

It appears that wherever this eternal place is, we're below it. There also seems to be a lot more going on *up there* than harp-playing on hammocks made of clouds. However, I recognize that I'm not meant to know everything (or even much) about eternity in this present existence. In fact, 1 Corinthians 2:9 (in discussing the crucifixion of Jesus) reminds us, '...as it is written, "What no eye has seen, nor ear heard, nor the heart of man imagined, what God has prepared for those who love him'--" So, let's stick to what we are experiencing in *this* realm, and explore what the

Bible says about those experiences.

Finally, it's worth noting that it's possible to gather a somewhat unhealthy obsession with the supernatural. Watch out for this trap. When taking on these topics, be careful to take everything back to Scripture. If you learn more about God and draw closer to Jesus in these studies, that's fantastic. However, if you find yourself "having itching ears" and you begin wandering "off into myths," or you find yourself confused -- remember that God is not the author of confusion (1 Cor. 14:33) and that it's important to avoid false teachers.

We are living in a unique era. Questions about the occult, aliens, and the like are expected and understandable. This book seeks to edify the church with answers to such questions -- but it is not, nor will it ever be, as important as the Gospel of Jesus Christ.

Odd Topic #1: Ghosts & Conversations With the Dead

Ghost stories are told for a lot of different reasons. Some cultures tell ghost stories for fun, while others share their legends as warnings. A certain number of ghost stories might be believed or, at the very least, reveal more questions than answers; while others are scoffed at -- shuffled to the back of mental folders labeled, "Useless Banter and Farfetched Yarns." There are too many anecdotes and myths spanning time and cultures to categorize them all in a single chapter. However, from widespread legends and literary works to cinematic productions, tales of strange sounds, moving objects, and apparitions are common fodder for the human intellect. So, the mind of an inquisitive Christian may wonder:

Are there spirits wandering the Earth; and if so,

why should we avoid them?

Those who believe in ghosts would likely agree that specters and spirits reveal themselves in many different ways. One person may describe their only encounter with a ghostly presence as the belief that small objects in their house have been repeatedly moved by an unseen force. Others may recollect sensing an obvious presence in one room of a building, but not in other spaces. Many describe hearing an incorporeal voice, along with its movements; and even children will play games like "Bloody Mary," convinced that *someone* saw *something* in a mirror at *some* point in time. There are individuals who will consult mediums and seek a word from lost loved ones; and sometimes, the grieving will recall a visitor in a dream. Since visits from the dead, poltergeists, and apparitions don't fully encompass the diversity of such phenomenon, perhaps we can start by narrowing it down to one question: Do spirits exist?

If one believes the Bible to be the inerrant Word of God, then it's reasonable to assume that the Bible's thoughts on the spiritual realm are true. (If someone reading this book feels otherwise, then I encourage them to study the validity of the Bible. There are many resources that delve into this matter, of which the author of this book has already researched and is therefore convinced that it is all together trustworthy.) Some may be surprised to learn that the Bible has a lot to say about spirits.

Take 1 Samuel, chapter 28, for example. Here we are told that King Saul sought out a medium -- the witch of Endor. He told her, "Bring up Samuel for me" (*ESV*, 1 Sam. 28.11). In short, she did so and said, "I see a god coming up out of the earth." Then Saul asked her, "'What is his appearance?" And she said, "An old man is coming up, and he is wrapped in a robe." And Saul knew that it was Samuel, and he bowed with his face to the ground and paid homage' (*ESV*, 1 Sam. 28.11-14).

Honestly, I'm not certain as to why Samuel came up out of the earth, or why he appeared old; but, I find it fascinating that the Bible describes this event. Samuel even asks, "Why have you disturbed me by bringing me up?" and goes on to tell Saul some bad news (1 Sam. 28.15).

However, notice the lack of popular stereotypes in this story. We learn that the witch is hiding her *ability* for fear of punishment. We also see her tend to Saul after the conversation with Samuel, because an intense fear has enfeebled him and left him without an appetite. She isn't hanging out in a dirty cave by a cauldron -- with a jar of bat wings, a green face, and a wart on the end of her nose -- waiting for a victim. Not everyone that conjures up spirits is kin to the Wicked Witch of the West. However, it's important to recognize that the Bible is clear about whether (or not) meddling with the dead is okay.

So, let's explore the Bible's definition of the spirit in this story. In verse 8 of this same chapter, Saul tells the medium, "Divine for me by a spirit and bring up for me whomever I shall name to you." In the King James Version, it reads, "...divine unto me by the familiar spirit, and bring me him up, whom I shall name unto thee." The word *spirit*, in this instance, is translated from Hebrew in the Strong's Concordance as:

A mumble, i.e. a water-skin (from its hollow sound); hence a necromancer (ventriloquist, as from a jar):--bottle, familiar spirit.

Even the word, *divine*, is associated with magic when written in Hebrew (Strong). Therefore, here we have a case of "magic" being used BY a familiar spirit to bring someone up. The *someone* (Samuel) is not solidly defined as the same type of spirit as the one doing the *divining*. The woman, the Witch of Endor, is the hollow shell that said spirit is using. It's easy to read through this story and think that the woman is calling up Samuel, but she is actually being used by a familiar spirit that is not Samuel.

In the Book of Isaiah, chapter 8 verses 19-20 read:

And when they say to you, "Inquire of the mediums and the necromancers who chirp and mutter," should not a people inquire of their God? Should they inquire of the dead on behalf of the living? To the teaching and to the testimony! If they will not speak according to this word, it is because they have no dawn.

Deuteronomy 18, verses 10-12 warns:

There shall not be found among you anyone who burns his son or his daughter as an offering, anyone who practices divination or tells fortunes or interprets omens, or a sorcerer or a charmer or a medium or a necromancer or one who inquires of the dead, for whoever does these things is an abomination to the Lord. And because of these abominations the Lord your God is driving them out before you.

Biblically speaking, it's clear that calling up the

dead personally, or via a "professional," is seriously frowned upon. Why, though? Why are mediums considered abominations? Most followers of the occult feel that they have been given special insight into how the spiritual realm works; and when a person accepts Jesus Christ as their Savior, they are told that they become *indwelled* by the Holy Spirit. They are taught to be vessels that the Holy Spirit can use to share the Gospel and the love of Christ with others.

Thus, we have a choice to make. Do we want to be used by the Holy Spirit? Or do we allow ourselves to be used by another spirit? Furthermore, what is that other spirit, if not holy?

For example, 1 Timothy 4:1 says, "Now the Spirit expressly says that in later times some will depart from the faith by devoting themselves to deceitful spirits and teachings of demons..." Hence, it's possible that the *other* spirits are deceitful. Perhaps that's why they're abominable.

Their lies bring spiritual death to those that choose to follow the teachings of demons, rather than accept the love and forgiveness of Jesus Christ.

More Verses To Consider

Hebrews 9:27 tells us that "...it is appointed for man

to die once, and after that comes judgment."

Ecclesiastes 9:5 says, "...the dead know nothing."

Then, there's the story of Lazarus and the rich man in Luke 16. Both died and went to separate locations. Lazarus went to "Abraham's side." The rich man found himself in Hades. Interestingly, verse 26 in this story says, "And besides all this, **between us and you a great chasm has been fixed, in order that those who would pass from here to you may not be able, and none may cross from there to us**" (emphasis mine).

Therefore, if it's not Grandma moving the trinkets on the dresser at night -- who is? I'm not saying it's not Grandma, but I am saying it's important to recognize that there are lying spirits out there. Be careful. (Besides, Grandma would be a lot better off in Heaven than hanging out in my bedroom... Just sayin'.)

Obviously, we don't have all the answers. Deuteronomy 29:29 says, "The secret things belong to the Lord our God, but the things that are revealed belong to us and to our children forever, that we may do all the words of this law." Paul, though, warns us that "even Satan disguises himself as an angel of light. So it is no surprise if his servants, also, disguise themselves as servants of righteousness. Their end will correspond to their deeds" (2 Cor. 11.14-15). In Ephesians, he also writes, "And you were dead in the trespasses and sins in which you once walked, following the course of this world, following the prince of the power of the air, the spirit that is now at work in the sons of disobedience—" (Eph. 2.1-2). So, here we read about a spirit working in the "sons of disobedience." He can be disguised "as an angel of light," and let's not forget that Satan is only one character in this shady bunch.

To avoid falling into deception, take 1 John 4:1's advice: "Beloved, do not believe every spirit, but test the spirits to see whether they are from God, for many false prophets have gone out into the world." If there is an entire realm beyond what we can see, it would be easy to fall into an unseen trap. If I were trying to rescue someone, and liars were leading them into traps along the way, I'd find such things abominable too. That being said, here are some more verses about spirits, necromancers, and demons. Ultimately, you must decide (under the guidance of the Holy Spirit) how it all fits together. It is my hope, however, that this information will help you approach the subject of ghosts with a better understanding.

Leviticus 19:31, 20:6
(20:27 - Praise God for the mercy of Jesus Christ!
This is no longer done.)
2 Kings 21:6
1 Chronicles 10:13
2 Chronicles 33:6
1 Samuel 28
(Saul and the Medium of En-dor)
Matthew 8:16, 12:45
Mark 1:27, 3:11, 5:1-20
Luke 7:21, 16:19-31 (Lazarus and the Rich Man)
Acts 8:7
1 Corinthians 12:10
Colossians 2:8,20
1 Timothy 4:1
Revelation 16:13-14
This is only a small list meant to assist the reader in
their studies. There are many more verses about
spirits, both clean and unclean.

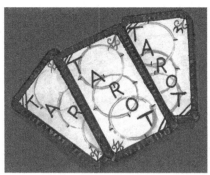

Odd Topic #2: Divination: The Good, the Bad, and the Unknown

On the Day of Atonement, Israel's high priest would enter the Holy of Holies, behind a thick veil, and sprinkle blood on the Ark of the Covenant. The blood came from sacrifices made for his sins, the sins of his family, and the sins of the people. He was the only one allowed to go in there, and there were a lot of things that had to be done before he COULD go in there. Otherwise, he would die.

I used to find the whole "sacrifice-and-blood-thing" very unsettling. As an unbeliever, I finally asked a pastor, "Why did Jesus have to die? Why did His blood have to pay for my sins? Why did it have to be blood that washes us?" His answer was a quote from the Bible, "...the wages of sin is death..." (Rom. 6.23). Even though our conversation that day led me to salvation, I still wondered, "Why blood?"

Obviously, I don't know all the intricacies of how the supernatural realm operates, but the rule about sin and death appears immutable. Sin leads to death. So, somewhere - something - has to die, because of the wage -- a payment for work that is done. In my studies, it became clear that life is in the blood, because Leviticus 17:11 says:

> *For the life of the flesh is in the blood, and I have given it for you on the altar to make atonement for your souls, for it is the blood that makes atonement by the life.*

Therefore, no matter how I would expect things to be done, this is the way it is. Life is in the blood, and it must be used to atone for sins. So, it was of eternal importance that the high priest entered the Holy of Holies once a year to sprinkle blood on the Mercy Seat and seek atonement for sins.

Incidentally, there were once cultures all across the globe that sacrificed animals (or even people) to pay their gods with blood. Why was this such a common practice, and (you may ask) what does this have to do with divination? How on earth does this information connect to my neighbor's deck of tarot cards? Hence, our next question:

Is divination in the Bible, and is it always bad?

There is great symbolism in the design and build of the tabernacle, the temple, its artifacts, and the priestly garments. The depth of it all would fill several books on its own. However, for our purpose, it's worth noting the curious thing that is carried in the garments of the high priest. He wore an ephod made "of gold, of blue and purple and scarlet yarns, and of fine twined linen, skillfully worked" (Ex. 28.6). There was also a square breastpiece bedecked with twelve precious stones. There was a ruby (sardius), a topaz, a garnet (carbuncle), an emerald, a sapphire, a diamond, a jacinth (which is a type of red-orange zircon gem), an agate, an amethyst, a beryl, an onyx, and a jasper. They were set in gold filigree, and each was associated with the name of an Israeli tribe.

Curiously, to us, there were two items placed inside the breastpiece called the Urim and the Thummim. (See Exodus 28:30 and Leviticus 8:8). There are different theories about how the Urim and Thummim were used, but no one in this era knows for sure. However, here is what we do know.

Urim means *lights*. We see the Urim alone in 1 Samuel 28:6.

And when Saul inquired of the Lord, the Lord did not answer him, either by dreams, or by Urim, or by prophets.

...and Numbers 27:21.
And he shall stand before Eleazar the priest, who shall inquire for him by the judgment of the Urim before the Lord. At his word they shall go out, and at his word they shall come in, both he and all the people of Israel with him, the whole congregation."

Thummim means *perfections*; and in the breastplate of the high priest, it represented complete Truth (Strong). The Thummim is mentioned, with the Urim, in Exodus 28:30.

And in the breastpiece of judgment you shall put the Urim and the Thummim, and they shall be on Aaron's heart, when he goes in before the Lord. Thus Aaron shall bear the judgment of the people of Israel on his heart before the Lord regularly.

It's also mentioned in Deuteronomy 33:8.
Give to Levi your Thummim,
and your Urim to your godly one,
whom you tested at Massah,
with whom you quarreled at the waters of Meribah;

Ezra 2:63
The governor told them that they were not to partake of the most holy food, until there should be a priest to consult Urim and Thummim.

Nehemiah 7:65
The governor told them that they were not to partake of the most holy food until a priest with Urim and Thummim should arise.

Leviticus 8:8
And he placed the breastpiece on him, and in the breastpiece he put the Urim and the Thummim.

...and 1 Samuel 14:41.
Therefore Saul said, "O Lord God of Israel, why have you not answered your servant this day? If this guilt is in me or in Jonathan my son, O Lord, God of Israel, give Urim. But if this guilt is in your people Israel, give Thummim." And Jonathan and Saul were taken, but the people escaped.

Judging by the verses in Ezra, Nehemiah, Numbers, and 1 Samuel, it appears that the Urim and the Thummim were used to pass along information to the people of Israel from their God. If divination involves seeking information from a supernatural realm, how can this be allowed?

Furthermore, what about Gideon and his famous fleece? The story of Gideon and the fleece is an example of a Biblical character seeking reassurance from God through, what could be considered as, divination. He's already heard from God, but his faith is shaking as he is under a lot of pressure; but, he is still seeking direction from the Creator of the universe and not some other entity.

First, I posit that divination is described as a sin because it's outside of the way that God provided. I don't know about you, but I don't have access to an Urim or a Thummim. We can read about divination being employed apart from God in 2 Kings, chapter 7. Notice the subsequent repercussions of such actions.

*They despised his statutes and his covenant that he made with their fathers and the warnings that he gave them. They went after false idols and **became false**, and they followed the nations that were around them, concerning whom the Lord had commanded them that they should not do like them. And they abandoned all the commandments of the Lord their God, and made for themselves metal images of two calves; and they made an Asherah and worshiped all the host of heaven and served Baal. And they burned their sons and their daughters as offerings and **used divination and omens** and sold themselves to do evil in the sight of the Lord, provoking him to anger. Therefore the Lord was very angry with Israel and removed them out of his sight. None was left but the tribe of Judah only* (2 Kings 7.15-18, emphasis mine).

Today, Jesus is our ever-present High Priest. When He died on the cross, the veil that separated everyone from the Holy of Holies was torn from top to bottom (Matthew 27:51), and His blood was the sacrifice to end all sacrifices. Basically, the separation between us and God was removed because of God's work in His Son, Jesus Christ. Now, we have constant access to God through Jesus. We can discern what direction to take via His

Holy Spirit and His Word, all while trusting our futures to Him. Should a need arise to tell us about the future, He will make that apparent. Otherwise, we take it day by day and let Him guide us through it all.

On another note, charlatans have claimed to see the future for centuries -- but some fortune tellers appear bonafide. Even the Bible mentions a slave girl with a "spirit of divination," but Paul rebukes the spirit and it comes out of her (Acts 16). Her owners were so upset over her sudden inability to tell the future, that they brought Paul and Silas before the authorities who, in turn, had them beaten and imprisoned.

All this to say, divination happens. It's not always smoke and mirrors. I remember, as an unbeliever, consulting Tarot cards for guidance or asking my Tarot reading friends to "do a read for me." I wouldn't have done this if I thought it was all nonsense. However, as we discussed before, "even Satan disguises himself as an angel of light" (2 Cor. 11.14).

In the Garden of Eden, the serpent said, "You will not surely die." No wonder the sin of divination is so frowned upon. It leads people astray in that it causes them to believe they don't need a Savior. If I were trying to rescue someone from a sinking ship, but they were told that my lifeboat was actually a shark (and that the sharks were lifeboats), I would be upset to see them swim away from the rescue ship. That, I believe, is the kind of lie we've been fighting for centuries - the lie that the remedy is actually the poison. It makes sense to a person who is turning to other gods -- false gods -- and in turn, they themselves *become false*.

One additional note...
    I do not agree that divination and casting lots are similar. Divination seeks information from an otherworldly source; but, casting lots often shows a willingness to accept whatever happens by chance. For instance, if I toss a coin in an effort to decide what I should make for dinner, I'm not seeking advice from some sort of mythical kitchen god.

More Verses To Consider

Here are some verses to consider regarding the position of the high priest, and also, Jesus as our High Priest.

High Priest: Heb. 2:17, 4:14-15, 7:26-27, 9:7,12

Anointing: Lev. 8:10-12; Isa 42:1; Mark 14:8

Torn Veil: Mat. 27:51; Mark 15:38; Luke 23:45

Holy Spirit: John 14:16-17, 14:26, 15:26; 1 Cor. 12:7-11; Jam. 1:5

Here is a passage about a different type of veil but with similar application. 2 Cor. 3:12-18

Here are some verses about the dangers of deceptive spirits.

You are of your father the devil, and your will is to do your father's desires. He was a murderer from the beginning, and does not stand in the truth, because there is no truth in him. When he lies, he speaks out of his own character, for he is a liar and the father of lies.

John 8:44

Be sober-minded; be watchful. Your adversary the devil prowls around like a roaring lion, seeking someone to devour.

1 Peter 5:8

Do not turn to mediums or necromancers; do not seek them out, and so make yourselves unclean by them: I am the Lord your God.

Leviticus 19:31

Here are some verses we already covered but that still apply:

Deu. 18:10-12, Isa. 8:19, 2 Cor. 11:14

Odd Topic #3: Is sorcery in the Bible, and why should we avoid it?

A lot of fantastic things happen in the Bible. Water parting, walking on water, turning water to wine... What about feeding 5,000 people with five loaves and two fish or giving sight to the blind? It's been said that what we consider magical may, in actuality, be something so far beyond our comprehension that we perceive it as magic. However, after leaving the occult and giving my life to Jesus, I had a *lot* of questions. So, I investigated as much as I could about the Bible's stance on sorcery and the occult. Since then, I have learned that the fight between good and evil is not an even-handed battle. Despite what yin yangs and fairy tales about the balance of the universe tell us, a huge deception is at play. The truth of the matter is that the Bible is full of extraordinary events, supernaturally affected by opposing (be they unequal) forces; and it consistently warns us away from the occult's deception for a reason.

Ergo, let's mark out what distinguishes sorcery from miraculous occurrences. Ephesians 6:12 reads, "For we do not wrestle against flesh and blood, but against the rulers, against the authorities, against the cosmic powers over this present darkness, against the spiritual forces of evil in the heavenly places." So, yes! There are spiritual forces of evil that have power, but God is all-powerful, all-seeing, all-knowing, and no one compares to Him.

In fact, did you ever notice that in the book of Revelation the devil is defeated in one verse? After years of hearing about him, like he's an equally important power, it turns out he's not. In one verse," …the devil who had deceived them was thrown into the lake of fire and sulfur where the beast and the false prophet were, and they will be tormented day and night forever and ever." (Rev. 20:10)

He's not part of some mythological deal, charged with keeping his supposed half of the cosmic scales balanced. He's not even the ruler of hell, despite what popular culture tells us; and look again at that part in Revelation 20:10 – "…the devil who had <u>deceived</u> them…" (emphasis mine). In the book of John, verse 8:44, Jesus says (of the devil), "…he is a liar and the father of lies." In contrast, Jesus says in chapter 14, "I am the way, and the truth, and the life. No one comes to the Father except through me." By "Father" Jesus is referring to our heavenly Father, God.

1 Kings Face-Off

When I read about Elijah taking on the 450 prophets of Baal and 400 prophets of Asherah in the book of 1 Kings, I admit, I sometimes hear Ennio Morricone's theme song, "The Good, the Bad, and the Ugly" playing in my head. In front of all Israel, Elijah challenges the people to make a decision. "How long will you go limping between two different opinions? If the Lord is God, follow him; but if Baal, then follow him." (1 Kings 18:21)

Then, there's this big showdown. Elijah tells the crowd, "I, even I only, am left a prophet of the Lord, but Baal's prophets are 450 men. Let two bulls be given to us, and let them choose one bull for themselves and cut it in pieces and lay it on the wood, but put no fire to it. And I will prepare the other bull and lay it on the wood and put no fire to it. And you call upon the name of your god, and I will call upon the name of the Lord, and the God who answers by fire, he is God." And all the people answered, "It is well spoken." (1 Kings 18:22-24)

Cue Morricone's famous song.

From morning, and into the afternoon, the prophets of Baal called on their so-called deity to bring down fire, but no answer came. They limped around the altar and cut themselves to the point that "blood gushed out upon them." Still, no fire appeared. The Bible says, "...there was no voice. No one answered; no one paid attention." (1 Kings 18:26-29)

When it was Elijah's turn to call out to God, he had them pour water onto the bull he had prepared and cut in pieces. In fact, he had them pour water over the bull and the wood 3 times! It's said that the water ran all over the altar and even into a trench. Then, after one prayer, "...the fire of the Lord fell and consumed the burnt offering and the wood and the stones and the dust, and licked up the water that was in the trench. And when all the people saw it, they fell on their faces and said, "The Lord, he is God; the Lord, he is God." (1 Kings 18:30-39)

I love that part. I can imagine it in my head, this fantastic scene where a bolt of fire slams into the altar in a fury of flame and sound. I can imagine the prophets of Baal and Asherah off to the side - sweaty, worn out and dripping blood - wondering what they did wrong. Then, they throw up their arms to shield themselves from the flash of a sudden and magnificent blaze, as fire from God lays waste the offering Elijah had prepared.

I mean, it appears that they truly expected their "little-g-gods" to respond. Why didn't they? Even in the Exodus account, Pharaoh's magicians asked their own false deities to perform magic, and things happened. So, why didn't these guys get any results?

To better understand what's happening here, let's go back to Exodus. Perhaps you recall when Aaron threw down his staff and it became a serpent. The pharaoh's magicians cast down their own staffs, while using "their secret arts," and they turned to serpents also. Then, Aaron's staff proceeded to swallow all of the other staffs, emphasizing the mightiness of Aaron and Moses' God. (Exodus 7)

At another point in the story, as the Lord commanded, "Aaron stretched out his hand with his staff and struck the dust of the earth, and there were gnats on man and beast. All the dust of the earth became gnats in all the land of Egypt." (Exodus 8:17) The magicians were unable to reproduce this effect. They told Pharaoh, "This is the finger of God." (Exodus 8:18-19)

Notice that the Pharaoh's magicians used "their secret arts" when they tried to copy what God did. Perhaps "their secret arts" consisted of spells, potions, blood, oils, and/or fire. Maybe it's written on a stele somewhere. I don't know, but they were trying to alter something in the natural world with natural tools, and hoping for a supernatural effect.

I find this interesting, because after leaving witchcraft, and becoming a follower of Jesus, I realized that I didn't have to buy any candles and herbs, or say any special words in a special way to get God's attention. The fact is, God doesn't need my help with anything. It's not just that He's more powerful than we are. I think it's also about the fact that He is not constrained by the natural world like we are.

In the case of Aaron, if God wants to use a staff, I imagine God can use whatever tool He chooses. Sometimes, He uses various tools and/or people; but, these often paint a picture that helps us gain a deeper appreciation of the Gospel. The first Passover is a prime example, with its blood on the doorposts and several parts of the meal itself - like the eating of unleavened bread. (See Exodus 12.) That entire event well depicts Jesus as the slain Lamb whose blood covers us and saves us from the power of sin and death.

Likewise, there are many occasions where God did amazing things without an instrument or person. In contrast, I never really learned anything from a burning candle. It just took up space and burned up oxygen. The question (I believe) is less about whether, or not, magic is real and more about where the magic is coming from.

In a previous chapter, we discussed the witch of En-dor from 1 Samuel 28. For more on the matter of familiar spirits and necromancy, see Odd Topic #1. However, in this segment we are looking specifically at apparent supernatural forces overpowering known natural forces; and we are considering why the sorcery found in these ancient stories did not always work. I propose that it's because those "cosmic powers over this present darkness," those "spiritual forces of evil in the heavenly places" (Ephesians 6:12) are inferior to the Lord God and will yield when He tells them to.

For some perspective, there's another story in Matthew, Mark, and Luke about a demoniac (two of them in Matthew's account). In Luke's account, it reads: 'Jesus then asked him, "What is your name?" And he said, "Legion," for many demons had entered him. And they begged him not to command them to depart into the abyss. Now a large herd of pigs was feeding there on the hillside, and they begged him to let them enter these. So he gave them permission. Then the demons came out of the man and entered the pigs, and the herd rushed down the steep bank into the lake and drowned.' (Luke 8:30-33)

Did you notice how the demons were begging Jesus to "let them enter" the pigs? Did you notice how He permitted them to do so? This large number of demons could torment men day and night, but they were no match for Jesus. They trembled before Him and begged. Time and time again, Jesus cast out demons. When He spoke a command, they obeyed. In this case, they recognized His authority and begged to be sent into a herd of pigs. Why He allowed it, why it happened that way, I'm still not sure - but the fact remains, this horde of demons could not contend with the Lord God of creation.

Earlier, I shared a story about a coffee mug that moved about, seemingly on its own, because of "magic." I mentioned that I now believe that coffee mug was being manipulated by demonic forces. By experimenting with magic, divination, and necromancy, I *went after false idols and became false* (2 Kings 17:15). I fell for the same kind of lies that the Bible warns us about, the same deceptions that people have been falling prey to since ancient times. However, since giving my life to Jesus, I am no longer strung along by lowly forces that are trying to take me down with them. I belong to the omnipotent, omniscient, and omnipresent Creator and loving God of the universe.

So, I'd like to reiterate Elijah's comment: "If the Lord is God, follow him." (1 Kings 18:21)

 To aid in your research, here are some more

verses about magic and sorcery.

Deuteronomy 18:10-12
There shall not be found among you anyone who burns his son or his daughter as an offering, anyone who practices divination or tells fortunes or interprets omens, or a sorcerer or a charmer or a medium or a necromancer or one who inquires of the dead, for whoever does these things is an abomination to the Lord. And because of these abominations the Lord your God is driving them out before you.

1 John 4:4
Little children, you are from God and have overcome them, for he who is in you is greater than he who is in the world.

Old Testament
Exodus 7-12
Exodus 22:18 says, "You shall not permit a sorceress to live." The Salem Witch Trials bother me terribly, because Jesus paid for my sins on the cross and theirs too (if any of them really were witches). I am reminded of the story of the adulterous woman who Jesus rescued from being stoned to death. (See John chapter 8, verses 1-11.) He paid for all our sins, those of the accused, and those of the accusers. Please do not condemn anyone to death.
Leviticus 20:6, 27
Deuteronomy 18:10-12
1 Samuel 28
2 Kings 21
2 Chronicles 33

Isaiah 47
Daniel 1:17-20
Daniel 2
Daniel 4-5
Malachi 3:5

New Testament
Acts 8
Acts 13
Acts 19
Galatians 5:19-21
1 John 4:4
Revelation 9:20-21
Revelation 21:8
Revelation 22:14-1

Odd Topic #4: Personal Anecdote, and a Word on Aliens

I've only met one person, in my entire life, that didn't know the story of the "Roswell Incident." It took me by surprise that something so deeply woven into today's social context could be missed, but alas - it was. So, I'm taking the chance that you've heard the story and will leave 1947 in the past. Let's consider the summer of 2002, instead.

By that July, I was already ankle-deep in the transmundane. The coffee mug (see An Encounter With a Coffee Mug), and a few other strange incidents between 1999 and 2002, left me with a sense that something was happening beyond what I could see around me. I wasn't a practicing witch, at that time, but I definitely had some questions.

So, the following story seems more curious to

me today than it did in 2002. In a manner of speaking, that time in my life is marked by a childlike race to recklessly throw open almost any spiritual doorway in a desperate search for answers. Then, along came another local coven with another alluring experience for me. I didn't seek them out. They just kind of "showed up" after I moved to Roswell, New Mexico.

I was invited to a tarot reading party. I'd never heard of such a thing, but it sounded intriguing. So I went. The party was held in a little run down shack of a house. A crowd of women filled the living room, and a middle-aged woman with long blonde hair did the readings. At one point, she announced that she would read for whoever could guess her middle name.

Immediately, a name filled my head. Lacking tact or any possible sense of hesitation, her name flew from my mouth as I spoke it aloud, and so they put me across the table from her for a reading. The entire thing left such an impression on me, that I went out and bought my own tarot deck from a local bookstore. That's when things really started to get hairy.

In high school, I had a small toy tarot deck that I bought at a clothing store in the mall. I read the little book that came with it, and another one like it that taught me how to read palms. I didn't want my parents to find the books. So, I hid them under my mattress. I tell you this, because I want to be honest in my testimony. The deck I bought in Roswell was not my first one - but it was the first one that I took seriously.

I took the tarot deck back to my dorm room, and per the instructions I had been given, I "got to know it." I don't remember what all that entailed, but I do remember that I was instructed to place it under my pillow as I slept. That's what I did.

Enter the Grays

We're told that "hindsight is 20/20" and indeed, it is. Looking back, I remember a night when I was woken abruptly as I slammed against my dorm room door. I was naked. My heart was pounding for fear, and my breathing was intense. If I were a character in a horror movie, and someone was chasing me with a chainsaw, that's what I would expect my reaction to be. I was looking out the peephole, but as I came to, I thought to myself, "What just happened?"

I turned on the overhead light, and hurried to the bathroom mirror. I had a trembling sense that I needed to see if I had been hurt, and I discovered that I was covered in scratches of varying shapes and lengths. I knew I'd been prone to night terrors ever since I bought my first tarot deck as a teenager, but I had never scratched up my back like that, and this felt so different. As adrenaline coursed through me, I sat anxiously, my back pressed against the wall at the head of my bed, and I watched – in case whatever had attacked me (if, indeed, that's what happened) returned. It was as if I knew that something evil had just happened.

The next day, I called my sister from a payphone and told her about it. We laughed, perhaps in an effort to lighten the mood, and joked about how I had just moved to Roswell. We quipped, "Well, it must have been the aliens!"

Shortly afterward, I started to get an upsetting pain in my abdomen. An ultrasound revealed an unknown space behind my uterus. Fearing that I was bleeding internally, emergency surgery was performed to find out what it was. It turned out that a cyst had formed behind my uterus.

The cyst removal was of little consequence to me, until recently, when I read the following section from Gary Bates' fascinating book, *Alien Intrusion: UFOs and the Evolution Connection*.

- *Abductees receive marks on their bodies other than the well-known scoops and straight-line scars. These other marks include single punctures, multiple punctures, large bruises, three and four fingered claw marks, and triangles of every possible sort.*

- *Female abductees often suffer serious gynecological problems after their alien encounters, and sometimes these problems lead to cysts, tumors, cancer of the breast and uterus, and to hysterectomies.*

He also notes that, "The most telling effects occur on the experiencer's personality and outlook on life or world view. It has been noticed by the majority of researchers that the person undergoes a type of religious transformation. They have also suggested that instigating a belief change in the abductee could be the reason for the whole enterprise. …the majority of abductees subsequently develop an interest, and openly participate, in New Age/occultic or Eastern-type mystical religions."

I don't recall being abducted by aliens, nor do I desire to. However, I do find it interesting that the incident occured when I decided to take the occult seriously.

That being said, perhaps you are wondering how I can possibly connect aliens and spirituality. Honestly, has it ever been that much of a leap? Even popular culture notices that there is definitely a link between people that have dabbled in the occult, and those who say they've been abducted by aliens; and just as people will scoff at the idea of sorcery, they will also scoff at the possibility that people are being abducted by aliens.

In fact, I wonder if the whole thing isn't even about aliens. There is a growing pool of literature that discusses the possibility that aliens are demonic entities, but instead of trying to convince you of that, let's see what the Bible says about our fourth odd topic...

Do aliens exist?

When God first created the heavens and the earth, everything was good. When Adam and Eve sinned in the Garden of Eden, everything started to die. We've already discussed sin, blood and redemption in previous chapters. So, let's take that information and read Hebrews 7:27...

He has no need, like those high priests, to offer sacrifices daily, first for his own sins and then for those of the people, since he did this once for all when he offered up himself.

...and Romans 8:19-22...

For the creation waits with eager longing for the revealing of the sons of God. For creation was subjected to futility, not willingly, but because of him who subjected it, in hope that the creation itself will be set free from its bondage to corruption and obtain the freedom of the glory of the children of God. For we know that the whole creation has been groaning together in the pains of childbirth until now.

Here we have two verses to consider when we explore the possibility that intergalactic space travelers exist. First, we're told that Jesus died "once for all when he offered up himself." Secondly, we read that creation is waiting, in its entirety, to "be set free" from sin and death.

We've talked about how Jesus took the form of a man and died on the cross to accept our punishment for sin; and that He makes the perfect High Priest because He can intercede on our behalf, knowing what it's like to be human. So, since sin entered by "one man," and by "one man's obedience" sin was paid for, who will be a high priest for the aliens if they are bound to creation in the way that we are? (Rom. 5:12,19)

Some say that the discovery of alien intelligence beyond our world will wreak havoc on the faith of many Earthlings. I beg to differ. There are those who will be taken by surprise, and we will see the foundation of their values radically shift. There are those that will believe that God must've made aliens too, and therefore, what's the harm? Then, some will believe it's a demonic deception.

I posit that the latter is the case. Why would God punish life on a distant planet for something one man on Earth did? Why would the current trend of UFO sightings and alien abductions appear so deceptive and mysterious? Why do people report a stop to alien abductions after accepting Jesus as their Savior, and why do "contactees" continually provide information from their extraterrestrial counterparts that is contrary to the Gospel, if it is not a ruse meant to deceive the masses?

The alien question can be a rabbit hole, if one isn't careful. Use caution, and don't forget that cultures across the centuries have shared stories about mysterious entities doing the same things to people, be they elves, fairies, demons, or goblins. In this technological age, we see aliens - but once upon a time, people feared other creatures of the night would abduct them.

Oddly enough, the topic of aliens requires more time to discuss. There's so many facets of it to cover (physics, quantum physics, historical anecdotes, legends, etc.), but that would take up an entire book.

At this moment, we know that, "...Christ has entered, not into holy places made with hands, which are copies of the true things, but into heaven itself, now to appear in the presence of God on our behalf." He didn't have to "offer himself repeatedly, as the high priest enters the holy places every year with blood not his own, for then he would have had to suffer repeatedly since the foundation of the world. But as it is, he has appeared once for all at the end of the ages to put away sin by the sacrifice of himself." (Hebrews 9:24-26) In short, who would pay for the aliens' sins if they need to be taken care of too?

Then, there's the question of all that universe out there. For anyone that thinks it would be a big "waste of space" to not have life on other planets, consider how incredibly loving our God must be when, even with all that space out there, He is so focused on our tiny little planet and our tiny little lives. Perhaps it's possible that the size of the universe not only *declares the glory of God* (see Psalm 19.1), but also conveys – in some way – the enormity of God's love and care.

Just For Fun: Odd Topic #5: Dinosaurs, Dragons, and Hippos! Oh My!

Once upon a time, I wanted to be a geologist. I had volunteered at a state park for two years, and studying the geologic formations of that park (excuse the pun) *rocked* my world. So, after high school finished, I became a geology major at a large university. As I mentioned earlier in the book, I was an atheist at the time. I was fascinated by evolution after reading Carl Sagan's *The Dragons of Eden*; and having read books like Darwin's *On the Origin of Species* and Hawking's *The Universe in a Nutshell*, I was convinced that the big bang and evolution were obvious answers to life's big questions. So it's not surprising that when I eventually *did* become a Christian, I had a lot of scientific questions. I mean, God gave us wonderful minds, and it's ok to ask questions. That's why one of the first things I studied was, "What happened to the dinosaurs?" It's a common question for young and old alike, and a valid question!

Still, this is going to be a short chapter. There's already so much information out there about this topic. I was floored when I discovered that there are many well-educated intelligent men and women scientists from all walks of life that do not believe the earth is as old as we've been taught in school. They have lots of information to share, and I encourage you to hear what they have to say; but beware of hoaxes and charlatans, who do a disservice to scientists of integrity. Sadly, they are out there - but there are also reputable places to look. The purpose of this chapter, however, is to think about what the Bible says - and that is all that I will cover here.

Job chapter 40 describes a very interesting creature. Here are verses 15-24:

Behold, Behemoth,

which I made as I made you;

he eats grass like an ox.

Behold, his strength in his loins,

and his power in the muscles of his belly.

He makes his tail stiff like a cedar;

the sinews of his thighs are knit together.

His bones are tubes of bronze,

his limbs like bars of iron.

"He is the first of the works of God;

let him who made him bring near his sword!

For the mountains yield food for him

where all the wild beasts play.

Under the lotus plants he lies,

in the shelter of the reeds and in the marsh.

For his shade the lotus trees cover him;

the willows of the brook surround him.

Behold, if the river is turbulent he is not frightened;

he is confident though Jordan rushes against his mouth.

Can one take him by his eyes,

or pierce his nose with a snare?

Different people define the behemoth as different things. Some say it's a hippopotamus. Some say an elephant. Some even say a dinosaur!

Let's look at this passage in pieces and see what we can discern from it. First, we are told that the behemoth "eats grass like an ox." So, we're likely talking about a herbivore. The hippo, the elephant, and plant-eating dinosaurs are still in the game; and before you ask, since the book of Job is considered to be very old, yes – even dinosaurs are a possibility from the standpoint of a young earth creationist.

Next, we read about Behemoth's powerful muscles and strength. Then, we see that "He makes his tail stiff like a cedar." Cedrus libani, or the Lebanese cedar, can grow between 40 and 130 feet tall. They can live over six hundred years and eventually reach a trunk diameter of 8 feet (Cedrus libani, 2022). In the King James Version of this verse about the cedar-like tail, it reads, "He moveth his tail like a cedar…"

That all being said, it's easy to see why many creationists think this describes the tail of a sauropod. According to guinessworldrecords.com, the longest sauropod dinosaur tail length ever recorded is between 43 and 45 feet. The elephant's tail can be as long as four feet, and the hippo's tail is flat and short. Still, this could all be hyperbole, and I'm not ready to give up on the elephant or the hippo. So, let's give them a "pass" on this one.

An example of a sauropod dinosaur and a hippopotamus, drawn by the author's daughter.

Let's look at the next tree mentioned in this passage. "Under the lotus plants he lies, / in the shelter of the reeds and in the marsh. / For his shade the lotus trees cover him…" Since lotus plants may rise a bit above the water, the amount of shade they provide left me wondering about the hippo - but the hippo's tail doesn't match the description. Regarding the lotus trees, I referred again to the original Hebrew word used in translating the King James Version which reads, "He lieth under the shady trees…" That word, *shady*, comes from a word that means "to be slender; the lotus tree:--

shady tree" (Strong, 6628).

One candidate for what was once identified as a lotus tree could be *Diospyros lotus*, the date-plum tree. It's native to southwest Asia and southeast Europe, can reach almost a hundred feet in height, and its trunk is not particularly wide (Date-plum, 2021). Such a tree would be able to provide shade for hippos, elephants, and sauropods alike.

Next, we read:

> *Behold, if the river is turbulent he is not frightened;*
>
> *he is confident though Jordan rushes against his mouth.*

In the King James:

> *Behold, he drinketh up a river, and hasteth not:*
>
> *he trusteth that he can draw up Jordan into his mouth.*

I'm not an expert in ancient manuscripts, though I'd really love to be; but, here we have one creature that doesn't find the river intimidating, and another version that can drink the entire river up.

At this point, I'm less inclined to believe that the behemoth is an elephant, but I can understand why some scholars believe he is a hippo. On the other hand, a sauropod fits all the descriptions, even the part about the tail.

If we pay attention to what's happening earlier in Job 40, we see the Lord challenging Job:

Have you an arm like God,

and can you thunder with a voice like his?

Adorn yourself with majesty and dignity;

clothe yourself with glory and splendor.

It's as if God is saying, "Do you compare to Me? If so, let's see your magnificence." Further down the passage, He challenges Job to humble the proud and *tread down the wicked.*

Then, God follows with this description of an animal called a behemoth. It has a tail like a cedar, isn't shaken by rushing waters, and rests under shady trees. In the next chapter, chapter 41, He continues by describing another beast called the leviathan. (More on that in a moment.) Hippos are interesting and all that, but do they really exude the same kind of majesty that - say - a supercell thunderstorm does? Or a giant dinosaur in the flesh? I'll leave this with you. Be it hippo or sauropod, I refer to Job 12:10: " In his hand is the life of every living thing and the breath of all mankind."

Whale or Sea Monster?

In Job 41, God continues His challenge as He describes a creature called Leviathan. I encourage you to read this chapter. Below I have added a couple questions in bold – things to consider…

"Can you draw out Leviathan with a fishhook

or press down his tongue with a cord?

Can you put a rope in his nose

or pierce his jaw with a hook?

Will he make many pleas to you?

Will he speak to you soft words?

Will he make a covenant with you

to take him for your servant forever?

Will you play with him as with a bird,

or will you put him on a leash for your girls?

Will traders bargain over him?

Will they divide him up among the merchants?

Can you fill his skin with harpoons

or his head with fishing spears?

There were ancient ways of catching a whale that didn't involve harpoons – like herding a whale toward a beach; but there is evidence that a harpoon could be used to attach a drogue to a whale, thereby wearing it down over time. However, traders could bargain over a whale, and whaling was happening way back in time (History of Whaling, 2022). So, if it's a whale, why ask such a question?

Lay your hands on him;

remember the battle—you will not do it again!

Behold, the hope of a man is false;

he is laid low even at the sight of him.

No one is so fierce that he dares to stir him up.

Who then is he who can stand before me?

I imagine that seeing a whale in person, out in the open ocean, is an awe inspiring

sight. Still (as far as whales go), there <u>are</u> men "so fierce" that they dare stir up such a catch. Let's skip down and take a look at the physical description we begin reading about in verse 14…

Who can open the doors of his face?

Around his teeth is terror.

His back is made of rows of shields,

shut up closely as with a seal.

One is so near to another

that no air can come between them.

They are joined one to another;

they clasp each other and cannot be separated.

Not all whales have teeth, but bristled filters could "look" like teeth I guess. On the other hand, whales have skin, not scales! What could this animal be?

His sneezings flash forth light,

and his eyes are like the eyelids of the dawn.

Out of his mouth go flaming torches;

sparks of fire leap forth.

Out of his nostrils comes forth smoke,

as from a boiling pot and burning rushes.

His breath kindles coals,

and a flame comes forth from his mouth.

In his neck abides strength,

and terror dances before him.

Whales don't have necks, either – and while this creature may just have really hot breath, it appears to breathe fire!

The description continues for another 12 verses and leaves little doubt that Leviathan is a formidable creature. Even figuratively, it's hard to make this animal out to be a whale. Some will say it's a crocodile, but the only way this seems plausible is if someone already adheres to the theory of evolution, and ignores the statement about Leviathan making "the deep boil like a pot" (v.31). Since when do crocodiles hang out in the ocean's depths? From a young earth standpoint, it's more likely this is a sea monster that is long since gone.

If there is any wonder about where this creature came from, see Psalm 104. Verses 25 and 26 read:

> *Here is the sea, great and wide,*
>
> *which teems with creatures innumerable,*
>
> *living things both small and great.*
>
> *There go the ships,*
>
> *and <u>Leviathan, which you formed to play in it</u>.*
>
> (Emphasis mine.)

Below is a sampling of more verses about monsters, dragons, serpents, and even the cockatrice. These words may be used interchangeably across translations. Also, keep in mind that serpents and dragons are sometimes used to describe something else, as in Jeremiah 51:34.

Behemoth
    Job 40
Cockatrice
    Jer. 8:17
    Is. 59:5
Dragon
    Is. 27:1, 51:9 ("habitation of dragons"… 34:13, 35:7, and 43:20)
    Job 30:29

Ps. 44:19, 74:13, 148:7

Jer. 9:11, 10:22 ("den of dragons")

Jer. 14:6

Jer. 49:33, 51:37 ("dwelling place for dragons" / hissing)

Mal. 1:3 ("dragons of the wilderness")

Rev. 12:3-4, 7, 9, 13, 16-17; 13:2, 4, 11; 16:13; 20:2

Fiery Flying Serpents

Is. 14:29, 30:6

Leviathan

Job 41

Ps. 74:14 (Possibly, and figuratively, referring to the escape from Egypt.)

Ps. 104:26

Monsters

Lam. 4:3 (sea monster or jackal?)

Serpents

Deut. 32:24

Job 26:13

Is. 27:1

Amos 9:3

Rev. 9:19, 12:9, 14-15; 20:2

Conclusion

The fantasy genre is a popular category of literature. On Sundays, I often drive past the local park, where a group of role players gather in their costumes to play their parts. I, myself, have camped out for tickets to a science fiction movie, and waited in long lines to see a new fantasy film. Maybe it's escapism that draws me in, but maybe it's also because we know there's something fantastic happening and we can't sense it on our own anymore.

Imagine how normal middle earth must seem to *Lord of the Rings* characters, while we see it as so exciting and imaginative. Referencing Charles Baudelaire, "...the cleverest ruse of the Devil is to persuade you he does not exist!" However, before Baudelaire's famous statement (originally written in the French language), a pastor named William Ramsey wrote, "One of the most striking proofs of the personal existence of Satan, which our times afford us, is found in the fact, that he has so influenced the minds of multitudes in reference to his existence and doings, as to make them believe that he does not exist; and that the hosts of Demons or Evil Spirits, over whom Satan presides as Prince, are only the phantacies of the brain, some halucination of mind. Could we have a stronger proof of the existence of a mind so mighty as to produce such results?"

Therefore, it is my conclusion (take it for what it's worth) that we are already surrounded by a supernatural, fantastic story. Some people know it. They see it, or they've gone looking for it; and when Christians aren't prepared with answers to their questions, those same people end up looking for answers elsewhere.

I, therefore, encourage the reader to not turn away from such subjects. As we are charged in 2 Timothy, chapter 4, "...preach the word; be ready in season and out of season; reprove, rebuke, and exhort, with complete patience and teaching. For the time is coming when people will not endure sound teaching, but having itching ears they will accumulate for themselves teachers to suit their own passions, and will turn away from listening to the truth and wander off into myths."

There is a grand, imaginative, magical story

taking place all around us. Don't miss it. Note the number of competing theories that span our human timeline and attempt to explain the nature of our existence. Truth is not relative. If it were, there would be no truth. Hence, there can only be one honest answer. That being said, don't be afraid to lean into these odd topics. Someday, someone you know may need to hear the truth.

The natural person does not accept the things of the Spirit of God, for they are folly to him, and he is not able to understand them because they are spiritually discerned.
1 Corinthians 2:14

'So Jesus said to the Jews who had believed him, "If you abide in my word, you are truly my disciples, and you will know the truth, and the truth will set you free."'
John 8:31-32

Works Cited

Bates, Gary. *Alien Intrusion: UFOs and the evolution connection.* Creation Book Publishers, 2010.

"Cedrus libani." Wikipedia: The Free Encyclopedia, 2022, en.wikipedia.org/wiki/Cedrus_libani

"Date-plum." Wikipedia: The Free Encyclopedia, 2021, en.wikipedia.org/wiki/Date-plum

Elephant tail: globalelephants.org/the-basics/

The Hendrickson Parallel Bible, Hendrickson Publishers, 2005.

"History of whaling." Wikipedia: The Free Encyclopedia, 2022, en.wikipedia.org/wiki/History_of_whaling#Early_history

Longest sauropod tail: guinessworldrecords.com/76061-longest-tail-on-a-dinosaur

Strong, James. *The New Strong's Complete Dictionary of Bible Words*. Thomas Nelson Publishers, 1996. Print.
>Divine (7080)

Strong, James. *The New Strong's Exhaustive Concordance of the Bible*. Thomas Nelson Publishers, 1990. Print.
>Behemoth (930)
>Heaven (8064)
>Leviathan (3882)
>Shady (6628)
>Spirit (178)
>Thummim (8550)
>Urim (224)

"The Greatest Trick the Devil Ever Pulled Was Convincing the World He Didn't Exist": https://quoteinvestigator.com/2018/03/20/devil/#:~:text=of%20the%20Devil.-,The%20greatest%20trick%20the%20Devil%20ever%20pulled%20was%20convincing%20the,Charles%20Baudelaire%20said%20something%20similar.

Made in the USA
Coppell, TX
04 October 2022

84065890R00039